KIDS will be KIDS

Published by Kids Will Be Kids
38 Baylawn Drive
Markham ON
L3S 2R8
Canada

ISBN - 978-0-9809382-3-4

Designed by: Sana Hashmi
Printed in China

Visit us at www.kidswillbekids.org

Daze of Fun:

Castle Park

Written By Nabeel Akbar
Illustrated By Anam Ahmad

"Ready to go to the park, Amanah?" my mom calls out.
"I'm all ready mom!" I reply with a shout.
Inshallah, we're going to meet some of my friends there,
Khalisah, Zainab and maybe even Seher.

Alhamdulillah, the day is warm and bright,
so mom decided to bring along my new red kite.

The park always has a lot of people around.
It has a big field, a pond and a playground.

In the large field people can have all sorts of fun,
playing sports, flying kites, or a picnic in the sun.

Some people bring their dogs and throw around a Frisbee
So long as they behave they're allowed to run free.
Some dogs leave a mess as they walk around and snoop,
But their owners are close behind to clean up their poop!

The pond has geese and ducks that you can feed.
Many people like to come just to relax and read.

The playground here is really enormous.
Shaped like a castle, it's colourful and gorgeous.
With slides and monkey bars, seesaws and rings,
tubes and spring horses, sliding poles and swings.

My friends are already here, a happy sight to see.
"Assalaamu-Alaikum!" they all greet me.

Sitting down with my friend's mothers, mom puts on her sun hat.
Our mom's all like to relax together and have a chit chat.
Seher claims, "they chat about us being so good and deserving applause."
"You Wish!" I laugh, "they're talking about all the trouble we cause!"

Zainab suggests, "let's go by the pond and have a sit."
"BOOORING!" says Khalisah, then shouts, "TAG YOU'RE IT!!"
She tags Zainab and runs into the castle park.
Zainab races after her like a wild and hungry shark.

It's a fun and tiring chase,
trying to tag someone in such a large space.

We laugh and run till our game of tag is complete, then continue exploring the castle park in the warm summer heat.

Later we head to the top to get on the biggest slide.
"watch me mom!!" I shout, and down I glide.

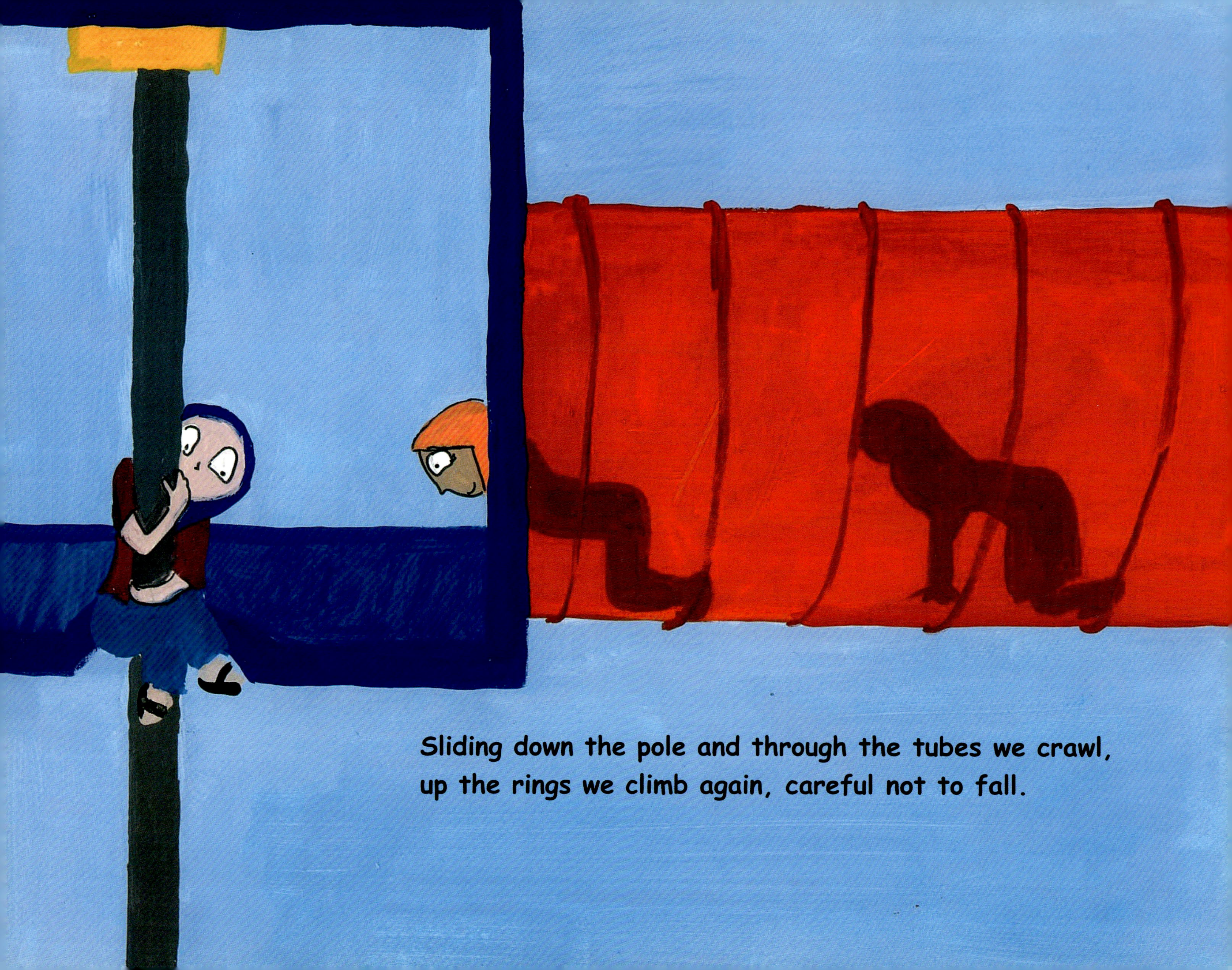

Sliding down the pole and through the tubes we crawl,
up the rings we climb again, careful not to fall.

We climb up some ropes onto a bridge that sways,
Then it's off to the merry-go-round, which gives us a daze.

If flying in the air is what we desire,
we get on the swings and swing higher and higher.

Always the brave one, Seher jumps while her swing is in the air.
There's nothing at all that this girl won't dare.

The monkey bars are something we haven't yet tried.
Over and under we climb, to get to the other side.

"Hey Amanah," says Seher, "please teach us how to fly your kite now!
"Good idea!" I say, "follow me, I'll show you all how."

I explain, "flying a kite can be done with ease,"
"especially today, with such a nice breeze."
"Mashallah," says Khalisah, "your kite is really neat."
"Yeah," agrees Seher, "getting to fly it will be a treat."

Zainab holds the kite as I begin to run.
"Bishmillah!" She throws it up, and now begins the fun!

Soaring and diving, we all watch it fly.
It looks smaller and smaller as it climbs in the sky.

Flying the kite, we each take a turn,
Zainab notes, "that was very easy to learn."

After some time our stomachs start to growl.
"Time For Lunch!!" I give a howl.
With our moms, we all have a picnic lunch.
Nothing can spoil the mood of this happy bunch.

We walk near the ducks and throw them some bread.
"Subhanallah," I say, "they look happy to be fed."

Its been a perfect afternoon, just like a dream,
And to top it all off, our mom's buy us ice cream!!

Glossary

Assalaamu- Alaikum - Peace be on you

Walikum Assalaam - And on you be peace

Alhamdullilah - All praise is for Allah

Inshallah - Allah willing

Subhanallah - Glory to Allah

Mashallah - It is as Allah has pleased

Bismillah - In the name of Allah

Amana - Faithful, to believe

Khalisah - Pure, clear

Seher - Beautiful sunshine

Zainab - Daughter of the Prophet Muhammad (peace be upon him)